Let's Build It!

By Larry Swerdlove

TREASURE BAY

Parent's Introduction

Whether your child is a beginning reader, a reluctant reader, or an eager reader, this book offers a fun and easy way to encourage and help your child in reading.

Developed with reading education specialists, **We Both Read** books invite you and your child to take turns reading aloud. You read the left-hand pages of the book, and your child reads the right-hand pages—which have been written at one of six early reading levels. The result is a wonderful new reading experience and faster reading development!

You may find it helpful to read the entire book aloud your-self the first time, then invite your child to participate the second time. As you read, try to make the story come alive by reading with expression. This will help to model good fluency. It will also be helpful to stop at various points to discuss what you are reading. This will help increase your child's understanding of what is being read.

In some books, a few challenging words are introduced in the parent's text, distinguished with **bold** lettering. Pointing out and discussing these words can help to build your child's reading vocabulary. If your child is a beginning reader, it may be helpful to run a finger under the text as each of you reads. Please also notice that a "talking parent" ☺ icon precedes the parent's text, and a "talking child" ☺ icon precedes the child's text.

If your child struggles with a word, you can encourage "sounding it out," but keep in mind that not all words can be sounded out. Your child might pick up clues about a word from the picture, other words in the sentence, or any rhyming patterns. If your child struggles with a word for more than five seconds, it is usually best to simply say the word.

Most of all, remember to praise your child's efforts and keep the reading fun. At the end of the book, there is a glossary of words, as well as some questions you can discuss. Rereading this book multiple times may also be helpful for your child.

Try to keep the tips above in mind as you read together, but don't worry about doing everything right. Simply sharing the enjoyment of reading together will increase your child's reading skills and help to start your child off on a lifetime of reading enjoyment!

Let's Build It!

A We Both Read Book
Level 1
Guided Reading: Level F

––––––––––––––––––––––––––

Use of photographs provided by iStock, Dreamstime, Fotosearch, and Shutterstock

We Both Read® is a registered trademark of Treasure Bay, Inc.

Published by
Treasure Bay, Inc.
P. O. Box 119
Novato, CA 94948 USA

Printed in Malaysia

Library of Congress Control Number: 2018950385

ISBN: 978-1-60115-308-1

Visit us online at
WeBothRead.com

PR-11-18

Table of Contents

Anyone Can Build!

Do you like to **build** things? Some kids like to build things with wooden blocks or plastic bricks. They might **build** a house, a bridge, or even a castle.

 You can **build** with sand too. But it will not last long.

⊙ Building a Home

In times past, people would build homes out of materials they could find nearby. Homes were built out of stone, mud, logs, animal hides, and even snow. Some homes are still built with these materials. Homes built from **cold**, hard-packed snow are called **igloos**.

Mud hut

Igloo

Teepees (or tepees)

You may see an **igloo** where it is **cold**.

You may see a mud hut where it is hot.

Build It Strong

Today, houses are made out of many different materials, including wood, bricks, concrete, and **steel**. Some homes are one-story structures. Some can be very tall with many floors, like apartment **buildings**.

Scaffolding for workers to walk on

6

Bricks

Buildings need to last. Tall buildings are made with a **steel** frame.

Tall buildings

Steel bars

Front-end loader

Backhoe

Bulldozer

Moving the Earth

In order to construct a building, the ground needs to be prepared. Many different types of heavy **machines** and equipment can be used to do the hard work.

Excavator and dump truck

This big **machine** lifts rocks and dirt. It puts the rocks and dirt into a dump truck.

Road grader

⊙ Even More Big Machines!

There are many other heavy machines used in construction. Excavators, augers, and backhoes dig. Graders smooth the dirt. Forklifts move materials. And bulldozers help move soil and rocks.

Drill rig

Forklift

If you want to dig a deep hole, a big machine can do it fast.

Excavator

Wooden frame

Concrete foundation

Pouring concrete for foundation

Start at the Bottom

You start building a house from the ground up.
Once you lay the foundation, you build the frame.
The frame is like the skeleton of the house.

These men are building the frame for a house. They build it with hammers and nails.

🔗 Tools You Hold in Your Hand

You need more than a **strong** hammer to build a house. Carpenters may also use saws, screwdrivers, tape measures, and drills. Some tools need electricity to operate.

Circular power saw

Hand saw

👷 You do not need to plug in a hand saw. You just need to be **strong**!

Power drill

Nail gun

Framing section

Who Builds All These Houses?

It takes many different people to build a house or other structure the **right** way. There are people who design it. Others pour the concrete for the foundation. There are also carpenters, plumbers, electricians, plasterers, and painters.

Spraying insulation into attic

Roofer attaching shingles

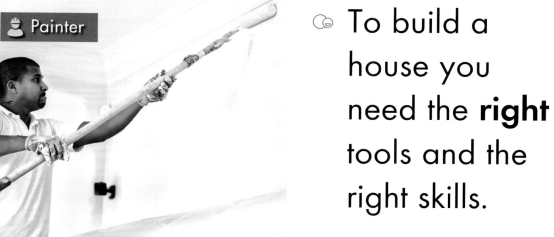

Painter

To build a house you need the **right** tools and the right skills.

Drywall finishing

Electrician

Floor plan

⊚ Draw It First

Architects are **people** who design buildings on paper and computers. They must think about what people will need in a building. They **also** must consider how to make it safe and pleasing to look at.

Architects create drawings of the floor plan for the building. A floor plan is like a map of the building.

Model of building

They may **also** make a model. The model lets other **people** see what the building will look like.

Skyscrapers under construction

⊙ Scraping the Sky

Skyscrapers were invented over 100 years ago. The tallest one is over a half mile high.

Most skyscrapers take years to build. On average they use more than 200,000 tons of **materials**, which is about the same weight as 44,000 elephants. That's more elephants than it would take to fill five football stadiums!

👤 Skyscrapers at night

👤 Steel bars reinforce the concrete for this building

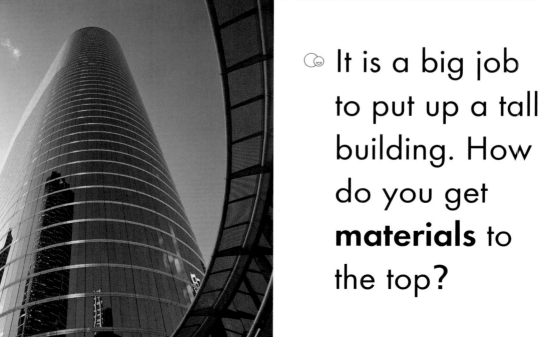

💬 It is a big job to put up a tall building. How do you get **materials** to the top?

Crane arm

👷 Build It Big

A **crane** is a **heavy** machine that can lift something into the air and move it somewhere else. To build a skyscraper, you need to lift things really high. That's what tower cranes are for.

👷 Concrete weights help balance the crane

👀 A **crane** can lift things that are very **heavy**. It can even lift other cranes!

23

Safety cable

Careful Up There

Safety is important on the job. Construction **workers** use the proper equipment and safety gear to prevent accidents. Many **workers** wear safety glasses. Steel **workers** must have good balance to walk on high beams, but they also usually wear safety harnesses.

Face shield

Safety harness

Boots

Hard hat

Ear plug

Workers wear boots and hard hats. Ear plugs help keep ears safe.

Open-air stadium

∞ Play Ball

One of the largest structures people build are sports stadiums. Most stadiums are open air. Where the weather is cold or rainy, some stadiums are built with a **roof**. There are even some stadiums with **roofs** that can be opened and closed.

Stadium with retractable roof

It takes a lot of cranes to put a **roof** on such a big building.

Stadium under construction

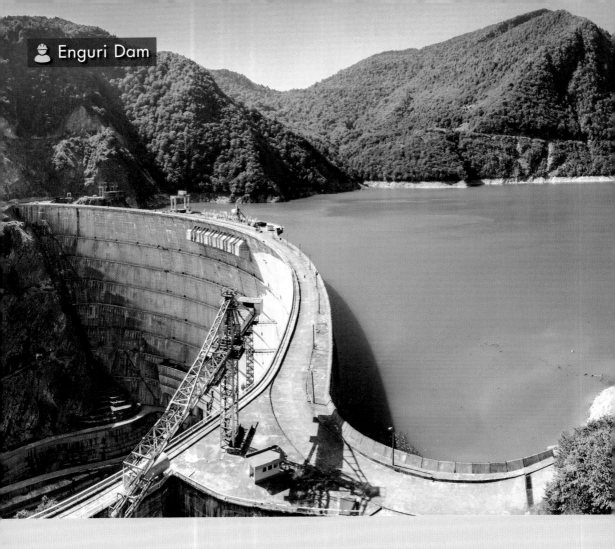

Enguri Dam

◎ Holding the Water Back

Some of the largest construction projects are dams. Dams block rivers and hold the water in a new lake or reservoir. This water can be used to help grow food on farms and even run through pipes into your home. **Many** dams are also used to generate clean electric **power**.

👁️ **Power** from a dam may help run **many** of the things in your home.

29

Wall of rock to be cut through by tunnel boring machine

⊚ Under Our Feet

Tunnels can help people travel quickly under cities, **through mountains,** or under a river. Many tunnels are dug using tunnel boring machines, which are sometimes called moles. These moles can be taller than a three-story house and can dig through 130 feet of rock and dirt every day.

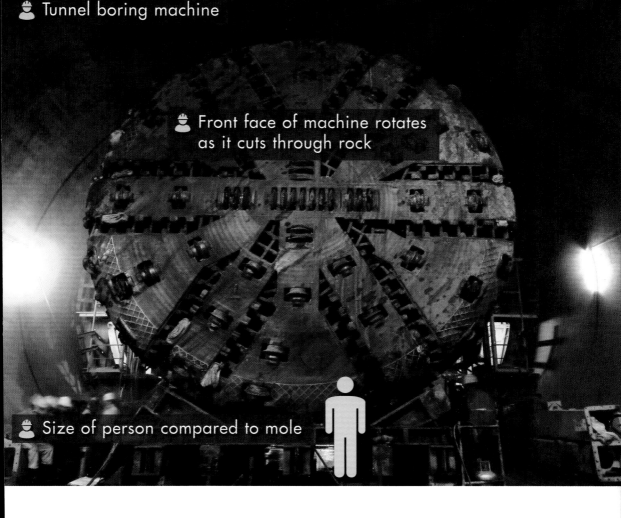

Tunnel boring machine

Front face of machine rotates as it cuts through rock

Size of person compared to mole

A mole was used to build a 35-mile tunnel that goes **through** the **mountains** in the Swiss Alps.

Bridge under construction

Concrete pylon

👤 Over the River

Bridges are a good way to travel over bodies of
water and deep canyons. Many bridges rest on large
support structures called pylons. Most pylons are
constructed of concrete and steel. Some bridges are
built on long wooden or steel poles called **piles**.

Pylon with suspension cables

Pile driver

This machine is called a pile driver. It slams the **piles** deep into the earth.

Asphalt box spreader

ꕺ Roads

Roads are built to help cars and trucks move **smoothly** and easily from one place to another. Many roads are built using an asphalt box spreader and other types of road-building machines.

Asphalt road rollers

Road-marking machine paints stripes

Road rollers make the road **smooth** and flat. Some people call them steam rollers.

Giant section of steel coaster being lowered into position

Hold On to Your Seat!

Roller coasters are made from wood or steel. Wood coasters are built from the ground up. Steel coasters are **bolted** together in segments.

Building a roller coaster can be as scary as riding one.

A big crane is used to lift each part. Then a worker must go up to **bolt** it in.

Excavator doing demolition

KEEP OUT
DEMOLITION
IN PROGRESS

👀 Look Out Below!

Sometimes an old building needs to be removed
before a new one can be built in its place. Bring in
the demolition crew! Some buildings are leveled with
explosives. If you want to **watch**, you have to stand
way back to be safe.

BOOM

1

2

3

4

Plug your ears. Ten, nine, eight, seven, six, five, four, three, two, one. Boom! **Watch** it fall.

⚭ You Can Build It!

Would you like to build something? You could use sand, plastic bricks, cardboard boxes, or even just two chairs and a blanket. If you would like to build something with wood, it's important to have an adult show you how to use your tools safely.

What **would** you like to build?
A dog house? A fort?
Or maybe a tent in your room?
Come on—let's build it!

Glossary

architect
a person who designs buildings and structures

construction
the activity of building something, or something that is already built

demolition
the act of taking something apart or destroying it—especially by explosives

excavator
a heavy machine that can dig deep into the ground

floor plan
a drawing of the rooms of a building as seen from above

material
anything used for building or making something

pylon
a tall structure used to support a bridge

structure
something that is built or constructed

Let's Talk about It

Add to the benefits of reading this book by discussing answers to these questions. Also consider discussing a few of your own questions.

1 Why do you think something built with sand will not last long?

2 If you could build something to play with, what would you like to build? What materials would you use?

3 If you could operate some big construction equipment, what kind would you like to operate? What could you help build with it?

4 If you could build a building that people could use, what would you like to build? What would it look like?

5 Why do you think people make models before building real buildings? Can you find the page that supports your answer?

6 What are some of the things you use electric power for? What do you think life would be like without electricity?

If you liked **Let's Built It!**, here are some other
We Both Read® books you are sure to enjoy!

To see all the We Both Read books that are available,
go to **WeBothRead.com**.